OUTRAGEOUS

LOVE

by Tony Seigh

Outrageous Love Ministries & Publications
Portland, Oregon

Outrageous Love by Tony Seigh

Outrageous Love Ministries & Publications
Portland, Oregon

This book or parts thereof may not be reproduced
in any form, stored in a retrieval system or
transmitted by any means - electronic, mechanical,
photocopy, recording, or otherwise - without prior
written permission of the publisher, except as
provided by United States of America copyright
law.

Cover Art and Layout by Benjamin Ewing
www.benewwwing.com

Such love has no fear, because perfect love expels all fear. If we are afraid, it is for fear of punishment, and this shows that we have not fully experienced His perfect love.

- I John 4:18

CONTENTS

ACKNOWLEDGMENTS

This book is a piece of me and the result of many conversations with some of my best friends on the planet, in particular, Blaise Foret and Austin Roberts (The Joy Boys). We have all spent many hours together reveling and drinking in the freedoms of this glorious good news together.

I also want to thank those who have deeply impacted my life through personal friendship or their written works and sermons, namely, John Crowder, Andre Rabe, Dave Vaughan, and Francois du Toit. The pioneering work of these men has so filled my heart with joy because of the good news they proclaim.

Thank you to all of our friends and partners who make our ministry possible and encourage us beyond measure. Above all, I want to thank my beautiful wife Kara and my family for being a constant support and always encouraging me to dream bigger.

INTRODUCTION
"WHO AM I?" AND "WHAT IS GOD LIKE?"

As I grew up in Portage, Indiana, an ordinary town along Lake Michigan, there were two questions that seemed to plague me, and I feel that every single person can relate to them.

The first one is, "Who am I?"

This goes back all the way to being a little kid, figuring out which sports, games, television shows, music, or friend group would define who I was. One year it was professional wrestling, the next football. One year I was really into punk music and I got a jean jacket with Rancid patches on it, but by the end of the year I was totally disinterested and had moved on to the next fad. I was always changing friends, changing interests, and changing hobbies because nothing really satisfied. Nothing made me feel fulfilled with my life.

I wanted something that was so uniquely ME... not just another amalgamation of pop culture, trends, or friend groups. So much of the energy of my life was spent attempting to fit in and find out the answer to this simple question:

Who am I?

My upbringing was interesting, but very normal by today's standards. My mom is an amazing woman who got pregnant with me as a teenager. My birth father is an Albanian man who was a small part of my life, but still never was 'Dad' in my eyes. Even though we shared facial features, I always called him by his first name. My stepfather on the other hand, who raised me as his own, this is the one I have always known as Dad. I grew up having a different last name than the rest of my family members. I didn't have my birth father's last name, or my stepfather's last name. I had my mother's maiden name. This may not seem like that big of a deal, but as an elementary school kid, it was a bit confusing. I wasn't sure exactly where I fit in. I remember wishing that somehow I could have my name changed so that I would fit in with the rest of the family. I wanted to belong. I was looking for my identity.

IDENTITY

Identity, we're all looking for it.

We long for that sense of belonging.

It's why we wear a Boston Red Sox hat or drink a certain beer. It's the reason behind Star Trek fan conventions and almost every niche of society. We all want to belong to something.

The feeling of belonging eluded me for years...

This rolls right into the second question; one which riddled me from an early age. The question is simply, "What is God like?"

This took different forms over the years.

Sometimes it was "Does God exist?"

At other times, it was a much more loaded question,

"If God is good, why does He let all this terrible stuff happen?

Why all the pain?

Why the death, destruction, war, and disease?"

I've always been a very existential thinker, I simply wanted to know the meaning of all this.

Are we just some cosmic soup that happened by chance?

Or is there something more?

These sorts of questions

about God

and life

and love

and eternity

and myself.

These questions are the ones I've had my whole life.

If you are a human being, *this book is for you*.

It's about you.

It's about the answer to these big questions that really define the life we know and live out.

Hour by hour,

day by day,

year after year.

THE ANSWERS TO OUR QUESTIONS

I'm not here to present to you a new ideology, or another theory, or ancient philosophy.

I have no interest in another religion, decision, or ritual.

The answer to these two questions, the questions of "Who am I?" and "What is God like?" The answer is one and the same.

In the climax of human history, the answer to these questions was revealed and burst forth on the scene.

Light was truly shining forth in the darkness.

Raw.

Real.

Tangible.

Flesh.

The answers to these questions have been melded into one.

Jesus has come as an example of you, revealing your perfection, union, and sonship. He has also come as a representation of God, showing us exactly the love, compassion, and heart of God. He reveals the true design for what human life is, in His perfect love and acceptance of us, and equally reveals these truths about God. Jesus came as the Son of God to show us that we are also the sons and daughters of His Father.

Fully human, fully divine, wrapped into one.

Never again would God and man be separate.

Never again would we have to fumble about in the dark at the questions of eternity and purpose.

God was now and forever would be flesh.

Human.

Just like you and me.

This is where we begin.

CHAPTER 1
LOVED BEFORE THE FOUNDATION OF THE WORLD

To understand who we are, let's go back to the beginning.

In fact, let's go back to *before the beginning.*

Before anything was even made.

Before we did anything good or bad.

Before we made a decision, or even took a breath.

God knew us.

God chose us.

God loved us.

"He chose us in Him before the foundation of the world, that we would be holy and blameless before Him" - Ephesians 1:4

Many have portrayed Christianity as merely another religion.

It's been marketed as one of the many belief systems out there that offer equations of religious duty, prayer, fasting, or good works to gain favor with God.

Jesus Christ came to show us something radically different than what any religion had to offer. You see, we don't merely end up in Christ…

Not through a decision

or ritual

or sacrifice.

We began in Him.

The best news ever is Jesus Christ. The gospel is a message that is not simply an idea or thought, but a Person. He tells us who we are and what God is like by revealing both of these truths in Himself as Son of God. He not only reflects the perfect likeness of God, but reveals perfectly who we are.

This is not a theory or idea, but God in human flesh.

We are God's family! Your Dad is God!

Mankind is indeed the very offspring of God, perfectly designed in the image of Jesus Christ...and when God dreamed you up, He didn't make a mistake.

"Do we not all have one father?
Has not one God created us?" - Malachi 2:10

Before there were any religions, belief systems, theologies, or philosophies, there was God, who is full of love and excited to share this love with a family.

This God, however, wasn't a lonely old man all by himself in some distant universe, but an unending, ever-loving community called Trinity - Father, Son, and Holy Spirit.

It is in the midst of this love community that we were fashioned and made to be adored forever by our Papa.

Jesus Christ didn't come to show us a way of intellectual ascent to believe in a God *out there*, but we now can see the fullness of God in the mirror, in ourselves.

The Word has become flesh and dwells in us.

When you meet Jesus, it is like meeting yourself for the first time. It's waking up from the dream of a false reality that says we are all alone, that we have no value, that we are a mistake. Jesus reveals our true value. He came and exchanged His life for us, becoming our sin and sharing His righteousness, because He saw value in us. The cross that He suffered was not to reveal how sinful you are, but reveals how valuable you are. Your freedom was His absolute priority, no matter what the cost.

He is a God who is in our midst, not a foreign intruder, but flesh and blood!

Jesus Christ came as the perfect expression of God, the exact representation of the Father, which is why He could boldly proclaim, "If you have seen Me, you have seen the Father."

God has found complete expression in human form.

We are bone of His bone, flesh of His flesh.

GOD IS WITH US

One of His names in the Hebrew language is Emmanuel, which means "God with us". You see, God became a man, made man fully in His own image, and invested all of Himself into mankind. This is the very reason that David, who was King of Israel, sang, "What is man that You think so highly of him?"

His name is "God with us", because there is no such thing as God without us!

The destiny of mankind has always been complete unity and enjoyment of God. This dynamic truth was revealed in Jesus, and He has not changed His mind at all concerning us.

He created us, not because God wanted more worship, or needed another creature to satisfy His ego (He doesn't have one). He wanted to make a creature that so exactly matches His own image, that He would have an equal partner to share the universe with.

This thought of humanity,

of the children of God,

this thought of you,

is the very thing that had God so excited to create the universe.

GOD HAS ALWAYS BEEN FOR US

Many have an idea of God, of His transcendence and holiness that makes Him un-relatable. It makes Him seem too busy for us, too holy for us, and disinterested from our pains and struggles.

Jesus reveals the truth about us and the truth about God. He came and showed us there was nothing wrong with God's design in mankind. Even though He was in the "likeness of sinful flesh", he didn't sin.

Even though humanity had lost sight of its identity and became captivated by so many wrong things, God never lost us or forgot about us. He came and reminded us that even though we had come to associate the human experience with sin, it simply was not the way things were meant to be.

So He showed us another way, *the way*.

The human body was the perfect vehicle for the love of God to manifest itself.

We see that even before Jesus died on the cross, as "the Lamb of God who takes away the sins of the world" (John 1:29), He had no problem interacting with sinful people!

He couldn't stand sin,

not because it offended His pride,

but because of the way it destroyed and confused His children.

On the cross, Jesus dealt with sin once and for all.

He cleansed us of all unrighteousness and made everything new.

"He has appeared once for all, at the climax of the ages to put away sin by His sacrifice." – Hebrews 9:26

THE ADULTEROUS WOMAN

We see in one of the most well known stories of Jesus' life His unconditional love and acceptance towards us.

There is a woman having sex with a guy that was not her husband and all of the religious leaders caught her red handed.

According to the Law of Moses, she should've been killed for committing such a crime.

Jesus simply said, "If anyone is without sin, let him cast the first stone at her."

Slowly, from oldest to youngest, everyone realized they had messed up too. But Jesus, who had never sinned, what did he do?

Did He stone and kill her according to the law?

Did He condemn her in her sin?

NO WAY!

He lifts her up, and says, "I do not condemn you. Go and sin no more."

The two things we learn about God through this story are nothing short of breathtaking.

First of all, we see that God does not condemn us!

He is a God that doesn't condemn us in our failure, which means we never have to live condemned.

Not even for another second.

Not after our greatest mess up.

Not even after a deep, dark sin.

We can fully trust in His acceptance of us, and have confidence, no matter what has happened, knowing that He loves us. This unconditional love for us in the midst of even the worst sin is the very power that makes sin undesirable.

As we awaken to the fact that God will never give up on us, no matter what we do, it sets us free to be ourselves. And as we taste the pleasures of the freedom that Christ revealed, it destroys the temptation to go back into the bondage of sin. It becomes as desirable as eating a fistful of dirt.

We are not condemned people and God is not one who condemns!

"The Son of Man did not come to condemn the world, but to save it." - John 3:17

"There is therefore now no condemnation for those who are in Christ." - Romans 8:1

Secondly, we see Jesus telling this woman to "Go and sin no more!"

How could this be?

A person caught in the midst of such adultery, surely, she would need to attend church for a while, get some counseling, and maybe do a special retreat or something before she'd be able to do that.

How could He expect this of her? Jesus, aren't you just asking for her failure?

You surely don't mean she can go and sin no more, do you?

Isn't she just a wretched sinner?

What about her wickedness?

It seems to me that Jesus knew far more about her, and us, than we had ever imagined. Although sin was real and a real issue that blinded us with shame and guilt, Jesus knew something more concrete and real about this woman and about us. He saw through the shroud of shame and saw a nature that went back further than sin.

You see if we are only looking back to Adam and the sin of mankind as our origin, we will be stuck thinking that we are dirty rotten sinners. But our true origin goes back farther, it's an origin found in God. We were crafted in His image and likeness.

Sin is not human, its inhuman.

The excuse of, "Well, of course we'll always sin, I'm just human" is a lie. God came as a man in the person of Jesus Christ and revealed that our design was not faulty or prone to sin. We were actually made for righteous living. We were made in His holiness and perfection. This is why Jesus could say to a woman that was just caught in adultery to "Go and sin no more!"

CHAPTER 2
JESUS: THE PERFECT PICTURE OF GOD

This is what God is like, exactly like Jesus.

He is not evil and does not delight in darkness.

This is true about all of us as well.

You may not fully believe it. You may not feel like it. But it is true.

Even though it may not feel like reality for you today,

It is the truth.

This is exactly why we are called to "set our mind on things above where Jesus is seated, not on the things of the earth."

Mankind is made in His pure and holy image, which is why sin just doesn't work. Living outside of the knowledge of His love and doing the things that hurt us and others are against our design. We feel the pain and hurt of it and even though it may offer a temporary sense of satisfaction, it never actually fulfills.

It doesn't fit.

It doesn't satisfy.

It always leaves us wanting more.

Sin is a foreign entity that entangled us for a while, but it was destroyed in Jesus' servant body on the cross

We can now know Him, even as we have always been known by Him.

It is in this knowing of Him that we discover our true selves.

You see, God has always known the true me, the child of God set apart in love and righteousness before the foundation of the world. But before I saw that about myself, before I saw what Christ had done for me, I lived a life of much lower quality because I didn't understand who I was. When we wake up to what God believes about us, a lightbulb switches on and we finally see ourselves and God as we both truly are.

We see that God is Love, and in His image, by His Spirit, we have become Love. This is why the rules and regulations of do's and don'ts can never compare with the freedom we were made for.

We were made to be lead by the Spirit, in a life of absolute love, joy, peace, and righteousness!

The truth is:

God has always been with us.

God has always been for us.

God has always been our Dad.

GOD NEVER GIVES UP ON US

I want to share with you my own story of God's faithfulness to me, even when I was completely faithless and didn't have strength to believe anymore.

It was the day before my 21st birthday on February 4, 2010 and I had recently moved across the country to 'seek God'. I thought if I could just get around other people that knew him, then I might be able to know him as well. Wanting nothing more than for him to be real to me, I had given up my full-ride at a university to pursue missions with hopes of getting closer to God. I remember hearing people talk about how God would speak to them, they would "feel his presence", and many seemed to have such a tangible relationship that I had never experienced.

On that day, I had just finished a Christian emotional healing seminar, and I felt the weight of my own brokenness. I remember thinking, "God, if I'm still this jacked up and your cross didn't take care of any of my problems, what's the point? Why did Jesus even die if it couldn't fix anything?"

I had given up a lot to get to this point and that day I decided that I no longer believed in God.

After two years of trying to be a Christian, I didn't want to be one any longer. I couldn't do it anymore.

I didn't understand all the Christian lingo, I had never grown up in church, and felt entirely alien to everything besides this man Jesus that I had decided to give my life to. That day, after all the pain and brokenness of my life seemed to come to a head,

I sat in a room,

with the lights turned off,

and wept.

I had lost so many friends after becoming a Christian.

I had isolated myself from many people to "pursue holiness", and now my 21st birthday was coming up and I had no one to celebrate it with.

And I wasn't even going to be able to go out and get drunk for my birthday.

I was still attending a Christian internship and that night I was supposed to go pray.

I didn't even know what to do.

I didn't know where to go,

who to talk to,

and definitely didn't want to be somewhere where I was supposed to talk to a God that I no longer thought existed.

At 11:45pm on February 4, 2010, 15 minutes before my 21st birthday, God spoke to me.

For the first time, I heard him.

I heard his voice.

Over and over and over again, he just spoke over me, "I love you. I am your Father. I love you. I am so proud of you..." It was more real to me than anything I had ever heard. Not only was it spoken, but it was felt. For the next 12 hours, I was in a supremely intoxicated state in the presence of God. For 12 hours, he was speaking to me and I was more drunk than I had ever been on any drug or drink in my past. It was like being on ecstasy and getting electrocuted and the most intense emotions I had ever felt...all at the same time. I couldn't snap out of it, and I didn't want to.

This same God who I no longer believed in, the one who I couldn't work up enough strength to live for, revealed himself to me.

I didn't even ask for forgiveness.

I didn't even like the thought of God existing.

And this God, my Father, told me I was his child and how much he loved me.

For the next week, I had trouble operating like a normal person. I was *intoxicated by this love*, by this experience, and I couldn't even function as normal. Over the next 6 months, I spent hours and hours a day in this state of ecstasy and joy. Many years of depression, self-hatred, suicidal thoughts, restlessness, and pain melted away in the bliss and joy of knowing Jesus. This was not merely an intellectual ascent of faith, but a spirit-to-spirit reality that was deeper than words. He embraced me in my rejection of Him.

I was consumed by this outrageous love.

Even if we have no faith, God is faithful.

Our Father accepts us before we accept Him.

He loves us before we love Him back.

He reconciled us before we believed.

He embraced us in our rejection of Him.

He took away our sins before anyone repented.

Before the world even began, He called us whole and innocent.

"Here is the extremity of God's love gift: mankind was rotten to the core when Christ died our death. If God could love us that much when we were ungodly and guilty, how much more are we free to realize His love now that we are declared innocent by His blood?" - Romans 5:8-9, Mirror Bible

CHAPTER 3
DEAD TO SIN, ALIVE TO GOD

We are no longer sinners.

Many of you have been told that you are merely forgiven sinners and will always struggle, and you just have to 'fight against it'.

Many describe the Christian life like we've been drafted into a battle and the spirit and the flesh are at war within us.

That's partially true.

The Spirit and the flesh are at war,

but not inside of you and me.

"You are not in the flesh, you are in the Spirit." - *Romans 8:9*

One of the most scandalous truths of what Jesus came and accomplished is this: **you are holy** and are **no longer a sinner**.

The Apostle Paul, who authored the majority of the New Testament, makes the points that we are 'dead to sin' and 'free from sin' dozens of times. He makes this fact clear in all of his letters, especially in the letter to the Romans.

A primary theme of his writings is the fact that Christ saved us single-handedly from all sin and made us perfect, apart from our efforts.

The scandalous news of the Gospel is that in one righteous act for everyone, Jesus made us holy on the cross.

There is no process of cleaning ourselves up, but Christ has made us whole,

delivered us from evil,

and we are fully 'inner healed'.

You may be thinking, "But why don't I feel whole? I feel like I still need a lot of cleaning up."

This is why I am sharing with you these truths today.

The truth about you is real whether you feel it or not,

believe it or not,

it's true.

But as we hear the Word, faith comes and we recognize that the reality we thought we knew isn't the full picture. Sometimes our perceptions of reality can become our reality, but the Gospel comes and tells us how perfect, holy, pure, and whole we are. It awakens faith in us to see it. As we hear how Christ has dealt with every problem, rather than trying to deal with it ourselves, or get more healing, we cast our cares upon him and thank Him that *it is finished*.

"Christ loved the church and gave himself up for her to make her holy, cleansing her by the washing with water through the word, and to present her to himself as a radiant church, without stain or wrinkle or any other blemish, but holy and blameless." - Ephesians 5:25-27

When Christ laid His life down for us all, dying on the cross, He removed every spot and stain. He made us *holy*, *blameless*, and *perfect*.

It was a perfect sacrifice on the cross for a perfect salvation.

"We have been sanctified through the offering of the body of Jesus Christ once for all...For by one offering He has perfected for all time those who are sanctified." - Hebrews 10:10,14

This is the truth about you right now, not some *future you* when you finally get your act together.

Jesus Christ did it all and He sees you as altogether amazing.

"You are altogether beautiful, my darling; there is no flaw in you." - Song of Solomon 4:7

You are dead to sin and alive to God.

Even though your body used to be controlled by sin, it has been crucified with Christ and sin was destroyed once and for all.

Your body is not a body of sin, but is the holy temple of God and your parts are instruments of righteousness.

"I have been crucified with Christ; and it is no longer I who live, but Christ lives in me; and the life which I now live in the flesh I live by faith in the Son of God,

who loved me and gave Himself up for me." - Galatians 2:20

PERFECTLY SANCTIFIED

You are *not* growing in holiness or sanctification, but Jesus has made you holy and has become your sanctification.

"By His doing you are in Christ Jesus, who became to us wisdom from God, and righteousness and sanctification, and redemption." - 1 Corinthians 1:30

You are not partially holy, or positionally holy. This is not just an idea or lofty thought, but a substantial reality, a brand new life.

You are perfect, through and through.

As He is, so are we in this world. - 1 John 4:17

Every part of you is full of light. There is nothing left in you that reminds God of sin because he has fully cleansed you of all darkness.

You are "just as if you never sinned". God was never keeping a record of your wrongs and any record that could've condemned you was nailed to the cross.

You are set apart, once and for all, in Christ. It is not a process of cleaning yourself up, but the reality of Christ's sacrifice.

We have been made whole in Christ, no longer controlled by sinfulness, but we are sharers in the divine nature. **You do not have a sinful nature.**

Paul shares this glorious truth that we are dead to sin and free from sin over 40 times in the book of Romans alone. If you still think you are a sinner, check out these scriptures:

*"What shall we say then? Are we to continue in sin that grace may abound? By no means! How can we who **died to sin** still live in it?"* - Romans 6:1-2

*"Do you not know that all of us who have been baptized into Christ Jesus were **baptized into his death**?"* - Romans 6:3

*"Therefore, if anyone is in Christ, **the new creation has come**: The old has gone, the new is here!"* - 2 Corinthians 5:17

*"We know that our **old self was crucified with him** in order that **the body of sin might be brought to***

*nothing, so that we would **no longer be enslaved to sin**." - Romans 6:6*

*"So you also must **consider yourselves dead to sin** and **alive to God** in Christ Jesus." - Romans 6:11*

*"When you came to Christ, you were "circumcised," but not by a physical procedure. Christ performed a spiritual circumcision — **the cutting away of your sinful nature**." - Colossians 2:11*

*"For **sin will have no dominion over you**, since you are not under law but under grace." - Romans 6:14*

*"But now that **you have been set free from sin**..." - Romans 6:22*

Are you noticing a theme here?

In Paul's letters, he gives us our death certificate to sin, and our birth certificate to life. And this is not just any life, but sharing in the life of God.

You see, you were once darkness, in your fallen understanding, but now you are light in the Lord. God simply couldn't co-exist with evil inside of you, so He made you full of light, full of Himself.

That same fullness of God that dwelled in Christ, is fully dwelling in you right now, and the sinful nature, that false identity that manipulated and controlled the human race, has been cut off once and for all. The old sinful you no longer exists, but was put to death with Christ on the cross.

*"For in Him the whole fullness of Deity (the Godhead) continues to dwell in bodily form [giving complete expression of the divine nature]. And you are in Him, made full and having come to fullness of life [in Christ you too are filled with the Godhead – Father, Son and Holy Spirit – and reach full spiritual stature]. And He is the Head of all rule and authority [of every angelic principality and power]. In Him also you were circumcised with a circumcision not made with hands, but in a [spiritual] circumcision [performed by] Christ by stripping off the body of the flesh (the whole corrupt, carnal nature with its passions and lusts)." -
Colossians 2:9-11 AMP*

The entirety of your corruption and carnal nature with its lusts and passions was circumcised. Circumcision is a one step process. That sinful self was ***cut off***, once and for all.

WHY DO I STILL STRUGGLE?

Some of you may be thinking? If I'm not a sinner anymore, why do I still sin? My question exactly, why *do* you still sin?

"What shall we say, then? Shall we go on sinning so that grace may increase? By no means! We are those who have died to sin; how can we live in it any longer?" - Romans 6:1-2

If you do sin, that doesn't mean your sinful nature was somehow resurrected. Adam and Eve when they were absolutely perfect in the Garden of Eden were tricked by Satan into sinning. The only power the evil one has is a lie. He tries to entangle us in lies about God and lies about ourselves. But I have good news:

"We know that no children of God keep on sinning, for the Son of God keeps them safe, and the Evil One cannot harm them." - 1 John 5:18, GNT

There is nothing wrong with us, but a lot of times wrong mindsets lead us into sin. If you are told you are still a sinner and have a sinful nature, of course you are going to struggle with sin. If you have a theology that keeps you in sin, then even though you fight it, you'll still end up sinning because you believe that it is part of your nature.

"However, if in our quest to discover righteousness by faith in what Christ did for us, we find that it is still possible to stumble; do not now label yourself a sinner yet again! The fact that you sinned does not cancel the cross of Christ and gives you no reason to abandon justification by faith as if Christ is to be blamed for your distraction! That would be absurd!" - Galatians 2:17, Mirror Translation

C.S. Lewis said, "You are what you believe." If you believe you are a sinner, you will live like it. If you believe you are righteous, you will live like it. Many fear that this Good News, with it's emphasis on the death of our sinfulness and our perfection in Christ, will somehow lead people to sin.

It's absolutely absurd.

You aren't a sinner anymore, why would you still live in it?

Telling people they are half saint, half sinner, is one of the only doctrines I know of that still gives people a license to sin.

You are complete in Christ,

full of Him,

perfect,

holy,

pure,

blameless,

and righteous.

"He who knew no sin became sin that we might become the righteousness of God." - 2 Corinthians 5:21

You are a new creature in a new world, absolutely sin-free, evil-free, and clean.

"For if a man is in Christ he becomes a new person altogether – the past is finished and gone, everything has become fresh and new." - 2 Corinthians 5:17

You are an altogether new person, perfected and clean in Jesus Christ. The old is gone and everything is new!

FREE FROM LEGALISM

There is nothing you can do to get any closer to God.

There is nothing you can do to make him love you any more.

There is nothing you can do to change his mind about you, for better or for worse.

He has already made up his mind about you.

You doing more acts of charity,

or reading the Bible more,

or going to church more,

or giving to the poor more,

or anything else you can think of,

none of this will get you one step closer to God or farther from God.

None of our religious or spiritual formulas matter to our Dad. In Jesus Christ, we have everything and He has truly done it all! He has secured us in every area of our lives, which is why as he died on the cross he said, "It is finished."

You don't need to pay Him back.

You don't need to earn His love.

Get over yourself and accept the facts.

He accepts you!

ALIVE TO GOD!

The Good News isn't primarily just freedom from sin or freedom from the law. While these are amazing benefits of the gospel, we mustn't just focus on what grace is not. Grace is not merely just freedom from sin and the law, but freedom unto an abundant life of bliss and satisfaction.

"Count yourselves dead to sin but alive to God in Christ Jesus." - Romans 6:11

Before religion and before sin, Jesus was there.

Grace must not find it's only definition as being "sin free" or "not the letter of the law".

While these concepts are valuable in setting people free from wrong mindsets, let us also move on to enjoy life in Christ! To understand God's grace we have to go back farther than the giving of the Law of Moses, and even the fall of Adam, to see the original intent of God the Father for mankind.

You see, before the fall of the world, before the creation of the world, Christ was there. And it was in Him that we were set apart to be holy and blameless before our Father.

If we are looking back to sin to find our origin, we need to look back further still.

Our origin is not in sin, but in Christ.

The Gospel is not Plan B.

It is not God's clean up plan for Adam's mistake.

Before Adam was formed or sin entered the picture, God knew us and loved us.

It was always God's intention for us to be redeemed by the blood of Jesus Christ. The Good News of Jesus Christ is an eternal truth that goes back forever. He is truly 'the Lamb that was slain before the foundation of the world'.

Long before Adam ever had a sin problem, God had a Christ solution.

CHAPTER 4
A WHOLE NEW WORLD IN JESUS

All of history was waiting for the crescendo of the incarnation of Jesus Christ. The prophets and the angels longed to look into this truth, to look into this glorious reality. They saw it in glimpses and shadow, but the full expression and radiance of God has now been revealed to us in His Son.

The cross of Jesus Christ is a manifestation in history of what God has believed about us all along.

This is how men like Enoch and Elijah tapped into the glories of a covenant to come, because in all reality, God had always seen us in the light of what Christ would come and do on the cross.

As Francois du Toit has said over and over again, "Before we were lost in Adam, we were found in Christ."

In Romans 5, we see a comparison between Adam and Christ. And even though Paul says they are not even comparable, he uses it to make a point. If death and condemnation entered and affected all mankind because of the single transgression of Adam, how much more does the one righteous act of Jesus Christ result in justification and life? The two are not even comparable.

The solution is even greater than the problem.

The sin problem has been dealt with once and for all.

In Hebrews 8, we see that Jesus Christ has enacted a new covenant with his own blood. He has set aside the old covenant of blessings and curses, and has enacted a new covenant. He has given us new hearts, forgiven all of our transgressions, and remembers our sins no more. He made one sacrifice for all, so that there would be no more remembrance of sin.

Jesus is the exact representation of God, and He is also the exact representation of man. He is proof that mankind was tailor-made to do good.

Everything that was lost in Adam has been recovered in Jesus Christ. We are in right relationship with God, a relationship that is guilt free, sin free, and full of love.

We have been restored to face-to-face communion with our Father.

The Gospel is the Good News of a Dad that wouldn't let anything get in the way of His kids knowing Him and experiencing His great love.

THE SHEPHERD OF OUR SOULS

What shall I compare the kingdom of God to? It is like a woman who loses a coin and searches all night until she finds it, and when she finds it, rejoicing, she tells everyone and celebrates!

What shall I liken the kingdom of God to? It is a like a Shepherd who when even one sheep goes astray, He leaves his 99 that are safe and sound to go and hunt that one sheep down. And when he finds it, He rejoices!

The same ones who were lost in Adam are now found in Christ.

From eternity past the plan of God has been for mankind to know and share in His glory and love. The destiny of mankind is to be forever a part of the Trinity, which was sealed in the fact of the Son of God becoming a man.

He became like us that we may be like Him!

You see, even though mankind was blind and had been distorted by sin, the intention of God never changed. His belief that we were His children never wavered! Not even for a second! He will never leave or forsake us.

The gospel openly displays the fact that God would rather go to hell and back, that He would rather die than live without us!

He had to have you!

You were the joy set before Him when He endured the cross.

No pain, no trial, no suffering could compare to the joy of redeeming your innocence and bringing you into right relationship with Him on the cross.

The Gospel is not another philosophy or do-it-yourself program, but is the reality of a loving

Father who refused to let sin, satan, or hell get in the way of a loving relationship with His kids.

I find it interesting that Paul, who "did not fail to proclaim the full counsel of God" only mentions the word "hell" one time in His writings and sermons. In 1 Corinthians 15, he asks,

"Death, where is your sting?
Hell (hades), where is your victory?"

Jesus Christ has destroyed the law of sin and death,

broken its power,

disarmed every power and principality,

and has brought us into right relationship with the Father.

ABUNDANT LIFE

Our life is now simple. Enjoy it!

We simply enjoy the abundant life He has given us.

We enjoy the bliss of our oneness with Him, and as we enjoy Him, it awakens all those around us to the fact that God is our Father. It reminds them of their first love. It awakens them to the One who formed them and knew them before they were even born.

The world is awakening to the fact of a loving Father, revealed in the person of Jesus Christ, revealed in you! Christ in you, the hope of glory!

The Gospel of Jesus Christ is JESUS CHRIST!

He is the mystic secret.

He is the mystery of the ages, it is Him!

When you meet Him, you meet yourself for the first time.

Our existence doesn't even make sense without Him because it is Him that reveals the truth about us. It is in Him that we live and move and have our being. He is the one who breathed the breath of life into our lungs and sustains us. He is the one who loves us and blesses us with everything we need.

It is in Him that we see the glory of God as in a mirror. Christ is in you! Look no further. You are now one with Him!

Even after faith and hope fade away, love will remain. God is love and now you are love because as He is, so are we! Our life is now a simple love affair with the one who made us, redeemed us, and enjoyed us from eternity past.

Jesus said, "On that day you will realize that I am in my Father and you are in me and I am in you." - John 14:20

Have you realized that you are included in this wonderful Life?

There's something about us that is so much greater than what law or sin has to say about us. He has redeemed mankind's true identity.

He redeemed the original intention for the human race in Jesus Christ.

Now we simply stand in awe of who He is and what He has done.

Jesus is our brother. He has brought us back to our Father who never gives up on us.

The thought of forsaking you has never even entered His mind.

This is eternal life: to know Him as we have always been known by Him.

There is an eternal love affair that God has with His children. He has invested all of Himself in us.

There is no going back.

You are His only inheritance.

You are His only desire.

And now you are His desire fulfilled!

The Gospel of Jesus Christ is simply the fact that His grace was enough to conquer sin and death and every other thing that could have possibly stood in the way of His children knowing His limitless love and unending bliss.

We can now experience the eternal life of knowing Him, freely and fully. He has given us life and life abundant and nothing can stop us from enjoying that!

Absolute freedom.

Unending grace.

Perfect love.

"I am convinced that neither death nor life, neither angels nor demons, neither the present nor the future, nor any powers, neither height nor depth, nor anything else in all creation, will be able to separate us from the love of God that is in Christ Jesus our Lord." – Romans 8:38-39

EVERYTHING WE NEED IN JESUS

As we look at how wonderful God is and what He has done for us, it removes the blinders that would make us think He is mean, angry, or withholding. His crazy love for us not only saved us from sin and brought us into a new life of righteousness, it also came with a pretty sweet perks package.

Many are afraid of being blessed by God.

"He did not spare his own Son but gave him for us all. So with Jesus, God will surely give us all things." - Romans 8:32

What does this mean, Tony? You surely can't be advocating the prosperity gospel?

The Gospel of Jesus Christ is far more offensive to the religious mind and much more prosperous than even prosperity advocates believe.

"The Lord is my Shepherd, I lack nothing." - Psalm 23:1

There is an unending supply of health, money, opportunities, and blessings that have been poured out upon us in Jesus.

He became a man of sorrows that we could be a people of joy.

He became poor that we might become rich.

He became sin that we could be the righteousness of God.

It is by His wounds that we are healed.

Jesus took all of our sickness, sadness, poverty, sin, depression, lack, wrong mindsets, and curses upon Himself so that we would be blessed.

He has already given us every spiritual blessing in the heavenly places. (Ephesians 1:3) Jesus knows that we have needs. You don't even have to be your own provider, but he provides everything you need. This is why Jesus said to simply "seek first the Kingdom, and all these things will be added to you". Just enjoy Him, get caught up in His love, and watch as He blesses your socks off.

Just like Abraham and Solomon, he wants to make you famously wealthy and prosperous, full of wisdom and good health.

FAMOUS FOR BLISS

A foreshadow of this great blessing that is for us was seen in God's covenant with Abraham:

Said the Eternal to Abram, "I will make a great nation of you and bless you and make you famous for your bliss…till all nations of the world seek bliss such as yours." - Genesis 12:1-3, Moffat Translation

You are a storehouse of blessing, absolutely filthy rich in Jesus Christ. As He is, so are you in this world. He is the King of Glory with all wealth, riches, health, and power, and you are one with Him!

God wants to make you famous for your bliss, a person that is so content with the finished work of the cross and secure in their identity that the nations come flocking to you to know Jesus. They will come to you to be blessed, receive healing, learn wisdom, and more.

Just like Solomon your fame will travel all over the world. This is not for your own glory or vanity or self-centeredness, but it is your rightful position as a child of the Most High God!

In Jesus, you are offensively blessed and it's not your fault! As you rest in Him, more fruitfulness than ever will spring forth from your life.

CHRIST IN US

"On that day you will realize that I am in my Father, and you are in me, and I am in you." - John 14:20

Christ is in us and we are in Christ! The fact of our being "In Christ" is the primary theological thrust of the letters of the apostle Paul. But what does it mean?

God is inside of you! You don't need to look for a God *out there* any more.

"This mystery has been kept in the dark for a long time, but now it's out in the open. God wanted everyone to know this rich and glorious secret inside and out, regardless of their background, regardless of their religious standing. The mystery in a nutshell is just this: Christ is in you, so therefore you can look forward to sharing in God's glory. It's that simple." - Colossians 1:27, MSG

Jesus did not come to just improve our lives and give us a clean slate at trying to live a moral life. **The Gospel is the absolutely foolish sounding proclamation that in His death, we have life.**

"For you died, and your life is now hidden with Christ in God." - Colossians 3:3

We now have a shared life with Him. We aren't waiting to one day go to heaven when we die, but all of heaven is inside of us! Jesus said, "The Kingdom of God is within you!" In fact, all of God is in you! Your old wretched sinful life has taken the plunge and you are now a sharer in the life of God!

"I am crucified with Christ: nevertheless I live; yet not I, but Christ liveth in me: and the life which I now live in the flesh I live by the faith of the Son of God, who loved me, and gave himself for me." - Galatians 2:20

Being in Christ is the most amazing state of being there is.

He is true reality,

true substance,

true life.

"This is eternal life, that they may know You, the only true God, and Jesus Christ whom You have sent." - John 17:3

Eternal life is not just the timeframe of a life that goes on forever, but also a quality of life that we share with Christ today. To live this life of Christ is to know true joy, bliss, peace, and contentment. There is nothing greater than this life He has offered us.

"The thief comes only to steal and kill and destroy; I have come that they may have life, and have it to the full." - John 10:10

This abundant life that is found in Christ is now yours and you are full of Him. The fullness of God is in you, you aren't working your way towards more. You can't get any closer.

Jesus is closer to you than your skin.

He is closer to you than your next breath.

You are one with Him and the fullness of God is inside of you and ready to be enjoyed.

You are complete in Him.

"For in him the whole fullness of deity dwells bodily, and you have been filled in him, who is the head of all rule and authority." - Colossians 2:9-10

CHRIST IN EVERYONE YOU MEET

My eyes have been radically awakened to the fact of Christ's reconciling work on the cross. Paul was out of his mind because of what Christ had done for all people, and it's truly been revolutionizing the way I see everyone and everything. I can't help but see Christ!

"If we are "out of our mind," as some say, it is for God; if we are in our right mind, it is for you. For Christ's love compels us, because we are convinced that one died for all, and therefore all died." - 2 Corinthians 5:13-14

In 2 Corinthians 5, we see "the love of Christ compels us, constrains us, possesses us."

Why?

Because "When One (Christ) died for all, all men died…therefore we now recognize NO ONE according to the flesh."

Because all died in Christ, we can no longer see people from a human point of view.

Every single person 'lives and moves and has their being in Him" and "we are all His offspring." (Acts 17)

Paul said all of this to pagans who worshiped many gods! Paul did not treat them as outsiders, but as included.

The gospel is not twisting someone's arm into accepting Christ, but it is the FACT that *"God was in Christ reconciling the world to himself, not counting men's sins against them."* - 2 Corinthians 5:19

Even though people may not know it, the facts are true.

The only existence there is to be had is in Christ and the gospel awakens men to the fact that God has already reconciled, loved, and forgiven them.

The gospel of Jesus Christ is not an invitation of what man must do to get right with God, but a declaration that Christ has already done it!

To repent is to awaken and turn to the fact that Christ has been "God with us" all along. Repentance is not an act that we do to earn favor with God. We see the Greek word *metanoia* that is translated to be the English word repent means simply "a change of mind" or "to turn". It is not something that we work up, but a grace that is granted as we shift from the illusion of sin and separation to the substance of everlasting life.

Every breath sustained,

every blessing given,

and every moment of love ever felt

has been given by the Father who knew and loved us before the foundation of the world!

When Paul was traveling on his way to persecute and kill Christians, *"God was pleased to reveal Christ in me that I may preach Him in the nations." - Galatians 1:16*

Before Paul even knew Christ,

even when he was vehemently opposing the Gospel,

God was pleased to reveal Christ in him.

Christ was in the murderous religionist Paul, but he didn't know it until He got knocked off his donkey.

What is my point here in saying all of this?

It is simply impossible for me to see any person as excluded from what Christ has done!

The whole world has been elected in Christ!

Every single human being is made in the image of God!

And before we were ever lost in Adam, we were set apart in Christ to be holy and blameless before him in love. (Read Ephesians 1 & 2)

If the transgression of Adam brought death and condemnation to all men, much more so did the righteous act of Jesus Christ bring justification and life to all men. (Romans 5:18)

We must see Christ as bigger than sin and separation!

Every person you meet, Christ loves! He desires that none would perish, but come to repentance. We must have hope for all people because God does.

When we see some as damned, excluded reprobates, it dehumanizes people that Christ died for. Every single person is precious and of infinite value in God's sight.

I cannot see anyone according to the flesh, but I see everyone according to what Christ has done.

He is a God that so loved the world! I look forward to the day when everyone 'remembers the source they came from' (Isaiah 51:1), realizes that 'there is one God and Father of us all' (Ephesians 4:6), and 'all the ends of the earth remember and turn to the LORD, and all the families of the nations bow down before him.' (Psalm 22:27)

My love for humanity, not just in general, but for every single individual I meet has never been so bursting within me. Everywhere I look, in every person, place, and thing *I see Jesus!* Let this ignite you as it did Paul. Look with eyes of faith to see a world loved by God.

UNTO THE LEAST OF THESE

To be with the poor is to be with Jesus. Every single thing 'done to the least of these, you do unto Jesus'. (Matthew 25) I'm so excited to see people everywhere awaken to the reality of a loving Father that has done everything for us! A generation will speak to one yet born that He has done it! (Psalm 22:31)

The Lord is opening our eyes as He did Peter who said,

"God has shown me that I should not call anyone impure or unclean." - Acts 10:28

Many of you may be wondering, "What about heaven and hell?" I have become utterly ignorant of everything except Christ and Him crucified. Jesus is not my ticket to a destination, but knowing Him is eternal life! Eternal life begins today, which is why I want to awaken all men to Christ.

Seeing the huge work of what Christ has done doesn't make me lazy or apathetic in regards to what men believe, but I have become *"out of my mind for God's sake" - 2 Corinthians 5:13*

I want everyone to believe and know Christ even as they have always been known by Him.

The gospel inspires worship and supplies faith.

His wonderful grace offers us a celebratory drink of reality that makes us drunk with love, yet at the same time sobers us up from the false reality that we could possibly live independent from the Lover of our souls.

Everywhere I go, the mystery of the ages is being revealed in people, *"Christ in you, the hope of glory"*. - *Colossians 1:27*

The idol of having it all figured out no longer matters to me at all. I have forgotten everything except Christ. Life is so simple now. He's everywhere I look. My life now consists of simple trust, absolute dependence, and pure love.

I look forward to the day when *"at the name of Jesus every knee should bow, in heaven and on earth and under the earth, and every tongue acknowledges that Jesus Christ is Lord, to the glory of God the Father."* - *Philippians 2:10-11*

RECONCILIATION

The work of reconciliation is a fact, not a potential truth.

Many have said that on the cross Jesus reconciled God to us, but we still need to reconcile ourselves to God. It's as though Jesus did his part to extend mercy, but now we have to do our part and make it happen. "God extended mercy, but you have to have faith!"

Our faith does not save us!

Jesus saves us!

"For by grace you have been saved through faith; and that not of yourselves, it is the gift of God." - Ephesians 2:8

It's His grace and His faith that saves us, it's all a gift from Him!

It's all His fault!

He is the author and perfecter of faith.

It's all Him from beginning to end.

God never needed to be reconciled to us. He has always been for us. The cross of Jesus Christ was not to change God's mind about us, but to change our minds about God. God didn't need reconciling, we did!

And this is exactly what Jesus did when He assumed our sin and responded to God on our behalf! Reconciliation is a fact. *"God was in Christ reconciling the world to himself, not counting peoples sins against them." - 2 Corinthians 5:19*

Because of all this, "be reconciled!" This doesn't mean you need to reconcile yourself, but be the reconciled person that you are! Live as a reconciled child of God. Be the true you that is revealed in Christ!

You are holy, therefore, live holy!

You are reconciled, therefore, don't waste another second in the lie of alienation from God!

As Winnie Banov has said, "The flat announcement of the Gospel turned out to be that God saves us singlehandedly. The saints were home before they started!"

ALL THINGS ARE NEW

At this point, I hope your eyes have opened to the fact that God has always loved us, He is way better than we ever could have thought, we are completely free from sin and bondage, and have been brought into a new and wonderful life. With such Good News of Christ's finished work, *what shall we do?*

Well, it's time to start deeply enjoying the life He has given us. It's time to enjoy Christ in us, with us, and all around us! He is everywhere we look and all things on earth and in heaven have been reconciled by the shedding of His blood.

"and through him to reconcile to himself all things, whether things on earth or things in heaven, by making peace through his blood, shed on the cross." - Colossians 1:20

We have truly become a part of a new world! We aren't trying to bring heaven to earth, but realizing that Christ has done it. Even though we may not have eyes to see, we are awakening to the truth of this glorious gospel.

"So if any man is in Christ, he is in a new world: the old things have come to an end; they have truly become new." - 2 Corinthians 5:17, BEB

Life is now an adventure in a new world of discovering all of the wonderful things Christ prepared for us. We have everything and we are going to be discovering more and more of what has already been given to us. We have barely even begun to discover all the riches and wonder available to us as the children of God.

Our lives are now simply to enjoy Him and let Him enjoy us as we walk in the good works He prepared for us.

We can rest in contentment and peace as we effortlessly see the world around us change because of who we are in Jesus. A sin free, love-filled, prosperous, healthy, Jesus driven life!

It's a dream come true!

He really is all that and a bag of chips.

The gospel is really unbelievably good, which is why he has to share His faith with us to actually believe it! It simply sounds too good to be true. Breathe deep, *you are free*.

This is just the beginning…

ABOUT THE AUTHOR

Tony Seigh is an author and speaker known for contagious joy, miracles, and the foundational teaching of the finished work of the cross of Jesus Christ.

As the founder of Outrageous Love Ministries, Tony travels all over the world preaching at churches, houses, and conferences, as well as doing gospel crusades, mission trips, and ministry to the poor. His greatest desire is to bring the gospel of Jesus Christ all over the globe through both preaching and loving on people everywhere.

Tony and his wife Kara enjoy living lives of ecstatic bliss, rest, and joy in Portland, Oregon.

Made in the USA
Lexington, KY
03 May 2014